SATURN

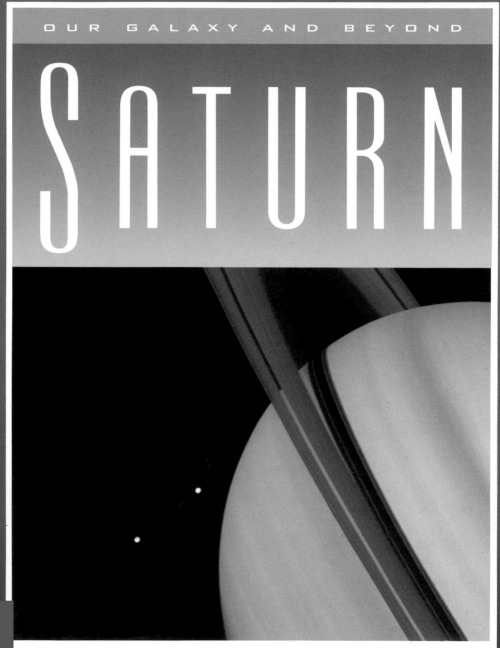

By Charnan Simon

Published in the United States of America by The Child's World®
P.O. Box 326, Chanhassen, MN 55317-0326
800-599-READ
www.childsworld.com

*Content Adviser:
Michelle Nichols,
Lead Educator for
Informal Programs,
Adler Planetarium
& Astronomy
Museum, Chicago,
Illinois*

Photo Credits: Cover: NASA/JPL/Caltech; Bettmann/Corbis: 4; Corbis: 5, 6, 7, 8 (Roger Ressmeyer), 15 (George D. Lepp), 17 (Chuck Savage), 18 (Reuters NewMedia Inc.), 24, 25, 26; ESA/Corbis Sygma: 11; NASA/JPL/Caltech: 9, 10 (J. T. Trauger/ Space Telescope Science Institute), 21, 27, 31; NASA/Roger Ressmeyer/Corbis: 13, 14, 20; Stocktrek/Corbis: 16, 22.

The Child's World®: Mary Berendes, Publishing Director
Editorial Directions, Inc.: E. Russell Primm, Editorial Director; Dana Rau, Line Editor; Elizabeth K. Martin, Assistant Editor; Olivia Nellums, Editorial Assistant; Susan Hindman, Copy Editor; Susan Ashley, Proofreader; Kevin Cunningham, Peter Garnham, Chris Simms, Fact Checkers; Tim Griffin/IndexServ, Indexer; Cian Loughlin O'Day, Photo Researcher; Linda S. Koutris, Photo Selector

Library of Congress Cataloging-in-Publication Data
Simon, Charnan.
 Saturn / by Charnan Simon.
    p. cm. — (Our galaxy and beyond)
Includes index.
Contents: Discovering Saturn—Saturn's atmosphere—What is Saturn made of?—
The rings of Saturn— Saturn's moons—How did Saturn form?
 ISBN 1-59296-054-5 (lib. bdg. : alk. paper)
 1. Saturn (Planet)—Juvenile literature. [1. Saturn (Planet)] I. Title. II. Series.
 QB671.S55 2004
 523.46—dc21   2003008040

TABLE OF CONTENTS

CHAPTER ONE

DISCOVERING SATURN

With its lovely rings, Saturn has been called the most beautiful planet in the solar system. For thousands of years, **astronomers** have studied its movement through the night sky.

The ancient Assyrians were the first to write about Saturn in 700 B.C. They named it after one of their gods, calling it the Star of Ninib.

Three hundred years later, the Greeks knew Saturn as Kronos. Kronos was the father of the Greek god Jupiter and was also the god of farming.

Later still, the Romans

Saturn gets its name from Saturnus, the Roman god of farming. The highest Roman god, Zeus, was his son.

Voyager 1 was 21.1 million miles (34 million kilometers) from Saturn when it took this image in October 1980.

called the planet Saturnas, which is where we get the name Saturn today. Saturnas was also a god of farming, and he was the father of the great Roman god Zeus.

In 1610, the Italian astronomer Galileo was the first person to see Saturn through a **telescope.** Galileo's telescope wasn't very strong. He couldn't see details very clearly. Galileo described Saturn as having "ears" or "cup handles" on either side of the planet.

Ancient astronomers learned about the planets by just looking into the night sky with their eyes. Starting in the early 1600s, however, scientists used telescopes to study the planets. By looking through a telescope, scientists could see planets in much greater detail.

Galileo was one of the first scientists to use a telescope to study the sky. He discovered amazing things, but Saturn puzzled him. At first he thought Saturn was really three planets—one large planet and two smaller ones on either side. His telescope simply was not strong enough to show that the two smaller "planets" were really Saturn's rings. In addition, these smaller "planets" seemed to disappear after several years—only to return again years later! Galileo wrote, "I do not know what to say in a case so surprising." He eventually decided Saturn must have "ears" that grew and disappeared. Galileo died without ever knowing the truth about Saturn's rings.

Today, scientists know why Saturn's "ears" disappear. As Saturn orbits, or goes around the Sun, its rings are usually tipped, making them easier to see. Every few years, though, we see Saturn's rings straight on, meaning we look right into the edge of the rings. The rings are so thin that it is very difficult to see them from Earth.

In 1655, the Dutch astronomer Christiaan Huygens saw that these "cup handles" were really a ring that went all the way around Saturn. Huygens also discovered Saturn's largest moon, Titan.

Twenty years later, a French astronomer, Jean Dominique Cassini, discovered a space in Saturn's ring. Could Saturn's ring really be two rings? Cassini also found four more moons surrounding Saturn—Iapetus, Rhea, Tethys, and Dione.

Hundreds of years passed. Telescopes got bigger and better.

Jean Dominique Cassini discovered the gap in Saturn's ring that is now known as the Cassini Division.

The first telescopes were small, handheld devices. Today, many telescopes are complicated instruments housed in huge domes, such as Yerkes Observatory, shown here.

Astronomers learned more about Saturn and the other planets that orbit our Sun. They learned that Saturn had still more moons. In fact, it has dozens. They also discovered that the ring around Saturn is not one ring or two, but many rings.

In 1980, the *Voyager 1* and *Voyager 2* spacecraft sent back amazing photographs of Saturn and piles of scientific information. After the Hubble Space Telescope was launched into space to orbit Earth in 1990, scientists learned still more about the ringed planet.

Today, we know a lot about Saturn. It is the sixth planet from the Sun and the second-largest, after Jupiter. Like Jupiter, Saturn is known as a "gas giant" because of its size and because it is made up mostly of hydrogen and helium gas. And Saturn IS a giant! More than 750 Earths could fit inside it!

Saturn is also the most flattened planet of all. All planets rotate, or spin. It takes Earth 24 hours—one day—to rotate once on its axis. The axis is an imaginary line between the top and

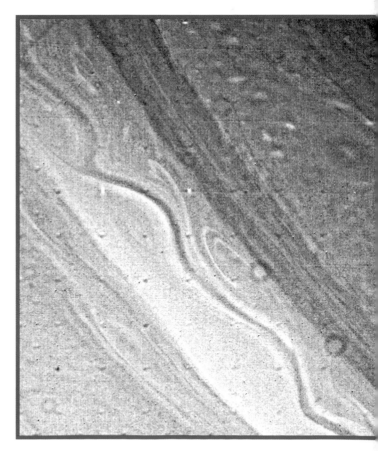

Saturn is a huge gas planet. The smallest items in the planet's ribbon-like cloud structure shown here are at least 30 miles (50 km) across. Scientists are working to understand how the planet's atmosphere is related to the ribbon and objects close to it.

The aurora glowing at Saturn's north and south poles add to its strange and mysterious beauty.

bottom of the planet, called its poles. It takes huge Saturn just 10 hours and 14 minutes to rotate on its axis. Saturn spins so fast, it bulges around its middle, or equator.

Saturn may rotate quickly, but it orbits slowly. Like Earth and all the other planets, Saturn moves around the Sun in a regular path called an orbit. Earth takes 365 days, or one year, to travel around the Sun. But Saturn is nine and a half times farther from the Sun than Earth. It takes Saturn 29 ½ Earth-years to go all the way around the Sun.

CASSINI-HUYGENS MISSION TO SATURN

Scientists still have lots of questions about Saturn. The *Cassini* spacecraft was launched in 1997 to help answer these questions. It will take *Cassini* seven years to even reach Saturn. Then, in 2004, the spacecraft will fly through a gap in Saturn's rings and go into orbit around the planet. *Cassini* will take hundreds of thousands of pictures and gather lots of information about Saturn, its rings, and its moons.

The *Cassini* spacecraft will also send a **probe** (shown above) called *Huygens* to land on Titan, Saturn's largest moon. *Huygens* will travel through Titan's thick clouds and then parachute down to the surface. It will gather information all that time. *Huygens* will hit the surface of Titan at about 25 miles (40 km) per hour. If it survives, it will send information to *Cassini* until its batteries run out. The *Cassini* spacecraft is about the size of a school bus. While in Saturn's orbit, it will take about one and a half hours to send its information back to Earth. Hundreds of scientists from all over the world will study its discoveries.

CHAPTER TWO

SATURN'S ATMOSPHERE

An atmosphere is the layer of gases that surrounds a planet. Earth's atmosphere is made up mostly of nitrogen and oxygen—perfect for humans to breathe. Saturn's atmosphere is mostly hydrogen and helium—NOT perfect for humans to breathe.

Through a telescope, Saturn appears to be a plain, hazy, yellowish-tan planet. It looks a little darker at its poles. Sometimes you can see a few darker bands stretching across its middle. Scientists know there are clouds on Saturn, but the layer of yellowish haze hides them.

The outer atmosphere of Saturn is cold. The average temperature is about –219° Fahrenheit (–139° Celsius). And Saturn is windy—very windy! At its equator, Saturn's winds can blow as hard as 1,118 miles (1,800 km) per hour. That's ten times faster than hurricane winds on Earth! These winds combine with the heat rising from the center of the planet to cause the yellowish-tan bands in Saturn's atmosphere.

Voyager 1 and *Voyager 2* sent back pictures of cloud swirls beneath Saturn's haze. The Voyager missions also noticed lightning

Saturn's yellowish appearance is a result of huge winds combined with heat rising from deep within its center.

on the planet. In September 1990, the Hubble Space Telescope showed a large patch of bright white storm clouds near Saturn's equator. Over time, scientists are learning more about Saturn's atmosphere.

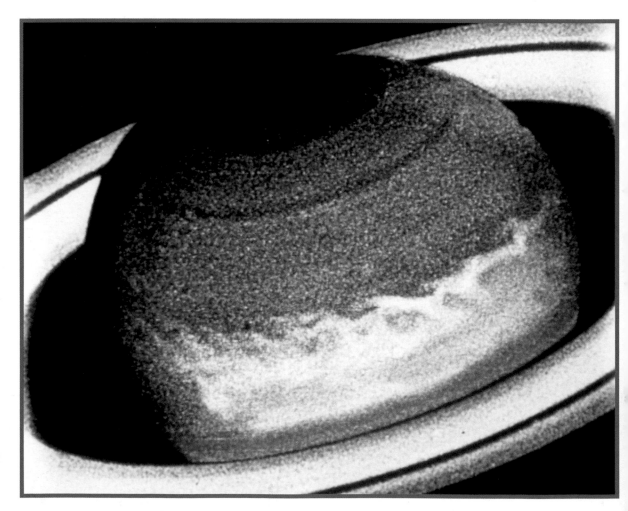

The white storm clouds that rage around Saturn's equator were caught in this photograph taken by the Hubble Space Telescope.

NORTHERN AND SOUTHERN LIGHTS ON SATURN?

Have you ever seen an aurora? They're beautiful to watch! On Earth, great, glowing, mostly green and pink lights streak and flicker across the wintry night sky near the poles.

To understand auroras you must first understand magnetic fields. A magnetic field is the area where a magnet's force can be felt. It is the area where a magnet works. Have you ever used a magnet to make steel paper clips "jump" off a table? They attach themselves to the magnet because they are inside its magnetic field. If you hold the magnet too far away, the paper clips will not move. They are outside the magnetic field.

Auroras are caused when **particles** from the Sun are trapped in Earth's magnetic field. Near Earth's North Pole, an aurora is called the Northern Lights (left), or aurora borealis. Around the South Pole, it is called the Southern Lights, or aurora australis. Scientists were excited when the *Voyager* spacecraft found aurora-like lights near Saturn's north and south poles, too. They are studying these auroras to learn more about Saturn and its magnetic field.

CHAPTER THREE

WHAT SATURN IS MADE OF

Saturn isn't anything at all like Earth. Earth is made of dirt, rock, and water. Its surface has mountains and valleys, rivers, lakes, and oceans. Saturn is made of—gases. It has no surface. That means there would be no place for a person to stand or for a spaceship to land. But there are differences between the layers of gas that make up Saturn.

The huge amount of pressure pressing down on Saturn creates these differences.

Saturn's atmosphere is made up of hydrogen and helium gas clouds. As the weight of these clouds presses downward, the gases get hotter and thicker. The enormous pressure of the atmosphere

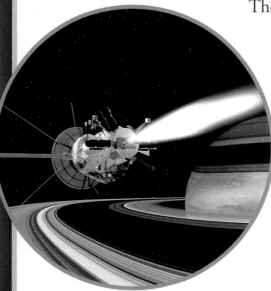

This orbiting spacecraft could never land on Saturn because the planet is a gas giant with no solid surface.

turns the lower layers of hydrogen gas into liquid hydrogen. Deeper still is a layer of liquid metallic hydrogen. Hydrogen gas can become liquid metallic hydrogen only at very high pressure. Movements in this layer are responsible for the planet's magnetic field. Saturn's center, or core, is made of melted rock. The temperature of the core is about 21,700° F (12,000° C)!

A scientist shows curious onlookers what liquid hydrogen is like.

A HOT MYSTERY

Saturn is a long way from the Sun. From Saturn, the Sun would appear ten times smaller than it appears on Earth. Saturn doesn't receive very much heat energy from the Sun. But something is heating Saturn. It gives off more heat energy than it gets from the Sun. Scientists think this energy comes from the way the helium and hydrogen gases mix together deep inside the planet.

CHAPTER FOUR

THE RINGS OF SATURN

When most people think of Saturn, they think of its rings. And who can blame them? Those marvelous rings have fascinated scientists and stargazers for hundreds of years.

The amazing close-up photographs of Saturn from the *Voyager* probes showed the planet's rings in detail. Instead of several large rings, scientists saw that there were tens of thousands of tiny rings, or ringlets.

These ringlets are made up of billions of chunks of ice particles mixed with rock. The largest chunks are as big as a house. Most are much smaller—the size of boulders, or snowballs, or even tiny specks of dust. Each chunk circles Saturn in its own orbit, like beads on a necklace.

Saturn's thousands of multicolored rings are so wide, they would fill up the space between Earth and the Moon.

Some of Saturn's rings look as if they have "spokes" in them. Scientists think these dark markings are really tiny pieces of dusty ice, held in place by Saturn's magnetic field. Other rings seem to be braided together.

Saturn's rings stretch 225,000 miles (362,102 km) from one side to the other. That is about the same distance as the space between Earth and the Moon. But the rings are very flat. They are only about 330 feet (100 meters) thick.

HOW DID THE RINGS FORM?

At one time, astronomers thought Saturn's rings might be ancient particles left over from when the solar system first formed. This would make the rings billions of years old.

Another idea is that the rings are broken-up pieces of one or more moons. These moons might have come too close to Saturn and been pulled apart by its gravity. Or, an asteroid may have crashed into the moons, causing them to smash into tiny pieces. If so, Saturn's rings may have formed only a few hundred million years ago.

Where did Saturn's rings come from, and how did they form? Scientists still don't know for sure.

CHAPTER FIVE

SATURN'S MOONS

Saturn is surrounded by moons. So far, 31 moons have been discovered. Saturn's moons are spread out all over the place. They range from 83,015 miles (133,600 km) to almost 8 million miles (13 million km) away from the planet. Some are icy with **craters** and valleys, while others have sharp, rocky ridges.

An artist's startling vision of the Ithaca Chasm on Saturn's moon Tethys

Scientists think the gravity from some of Saturn's moons keeps the rings from falling into the planet or spreading far into space. They call these special moons shepherd moons. Just as faithful sheepdogs keep a herd of sheep together, shepherd moons such as Pandora, Prometheus, and Atlas keep the rings orbiting smoothly.

Saturn's largest moon is named Titan. Titan is larger than any other moon in the solar system except Jupiter's moon Ganymede. Titan is even bigger than the planets Pluto and Mercury.

Scientists are not just interested in Titan because of its size. Titan is the only body in the solar system, besides Earth, that has an atmosphere made mostly of nitrogen. Scientists think Titan might be a lot like Earth was 4 billion years ago.

But Titan is hard to study. *Voyager 1* took pictures of Titan when it flew past. All it could see was a thick layer of haze and clouds.

Scientists know that Titan is too cold to support life. The temperature

on the surface is only about –289° F (–178° C). Scientists are looking

forward to 2004, when *Huygens* will fall through Titan's atmosphere

and try to land on its surface. They hope Titan will tell them a lot

about what Earth was like long ago.

An artist imagines the landing of a space probe on the moon Titan.

OTHER MOONS, OTHER STORIES

Titan is just one of Saturn's many moons. There are lots more!

The moon named Enceladus (right) is covered with smooth, clear ice. Almost all of the sunlight that hits Enceladus bounces right off its icy surface. This makes Enceladus the shiniest body in the solar system.

Phoebe is another interesting moon. Scientists think that black, sooty Phoebe was once a comet that passed too close to Saturn and was "captured" by its gravity.

Then there's Iapetus. One side of Iapetus is pure, gleam-

however, is a sooty black. It could be that Phoebe is trailing its space dust onto Iapetus. Scientists aren't sure what is happening on Iapetus.

Mimas has a giant crater that takes up one-third of the moon. It looks like a giant eyeball. The crash that caused the crater must have nearly blown Mimas apart!

Janus and Epimetheus are small moons that follow the exact same orbit around Saturn. Scientists believe they might be halves of one moon. This moon may have broken in two when it crashed with

CHAPTER SIX

How Saturn May Have Formed

Nobody knows exactly how Saturn, or any of the planets, formed. But scientists have a pretty good idea. About 5 billion years ago, a large cloud of gas and dust began spinning in space.

Saturn and the other planets probably formed out of a huge dust cloud in space. That cloud may have been similar to this one caught on film by the Hubble Space Telescope.

At the very center of the cloud, the Sun formed. Away from the Sun, tiny particles of gas and dust clumped together to form chunks. Some chunks formed planets. Those planets closest to the

Sun were made mostly of

rock and metal.

Farther from the

Sun, where it was

cooler, chunks of ice

combined with the gas and

dust particles to create large,

rocky bodies. At the same time,

the newly formed Sun was

Scientists have determined that the cratered surface of Saturn's moon Rhea is ancient. The moon probably came into being immediately after the planets formed, about 4.5 billion years ago.

blowing more gas and dust into the outer solar system. The large

bodies that would become Jupiter and Saturn grew large enough

to be able to pull in lots of that gas and dust with gravity. These

events created Saturn, a planet that continues to amaze us with its

beauty and mystery.

Glossary

asteroid (ASS-tuh-royd) An asteroid is a rocky object that orbits the Sun.

astronomers (uh-STRAW-nuh-merz) Astronomers are scientists who study space and the stars and planets.

comet (KOM-it) A comet is a bright object, followed by a tail of dust and ice, that orbits the Sun in a long, oval-shaped path.

craters (CRAY-tuhrs) Craters are large, bowl-shaped holes on a planet or moon caused by a comet, asteroid, or meteorite that hits its surface.

gravity (GRA-vuh-tee) Gravity is a force that pulls one object toward another.

meteorite (MEE-tee-uh-rite) A meteorite is a rocky, metallic object from space that hits the surface of a planet or moon.

particles (PAR-tuh-kuhls) Particles are tiny pieces of something.

probe (PROBE) A probe is a machine or tool that explores something.

telescope (TEL-uh-skope) A telescope is an instrument used to study things that are far away, such as stars and planets, by making them seem larger and closer.

Did You Know?

▶ Saturn is the lightest of any planet. It's so light that it would float on water, if you could only find a bathtub large enough!

▶ Saturn is twice as far away from the Sun as Jupiter.

▶ Seasons on Earth last about three months. Seasons on Saturn last about seven years!

▶ In October 1994, the Hubble Space Telescope sent back pictures that showed bright and dark areas on the surface of Saturn's moon Titan. Could they be large areas of land? Frozen oceans? Scientists are hoping that *Huygens* will help answer these and other questions about Titan.

Fast Facts

Diameter: 74,897 miles (120,535 km)

Atmosphere: hydrogen, helium

Time to orbit the Sun (one Saturn-year): 29.5 Earth-years

Time to turn on axis (one Saturn-day): 10 hours, 14 minutes

Shortest distance from Sun: 839 million miles (1.3 billion km)

Greatest distance from Sun: 938 million miles (1.5 billion km)

Shortest distance from Earth: 743 million miles (1.19 billion km)

Greatest distance from Earth: 1 billion miles (1.6 billion km)

Surface gravity: 1.16 times that of Earth. A person weighing 80 pounds (36 kg) on Earth would weigh about 93 pounds (42 kg) on Saturn.

Temperature range: –219° F (–139° C) in the outer atmosphere; 21,700° F (12,000° C) at the core

Number of known moons: 31

How to Learn More about Saturn

At the Library

Asimov, Isaac, and Richard Hantula. *Saturn.* Milwaukee: Gareth Stevens, 2002.

Haugen, David M. *Saturn.* San Diego: Kidhaven Press, 2002.

Kerrod, Robin. *The Far Planets.* Austin, Tex.: Raintree Steck-Vaughn, 2002.

Kerrod, Robin. *Saturn.* Minneapolis: Lerner Publications Co., 2000.

Margaret, Amy. *Saturn.* New York: PowerKids Press, 2001.

Sparrow, Giles. *Saturn.* Chicago: Heinemann Library, 2001.

Stone, Tanya Lee. *Saturn.* New York: Benchmark Books, 2002.

On the Web

Visit our home page for lots of links about Saturn:
http://www.childsworld.com/links.html
Note to Parents, Teachers, and Librarians: We routinely verify our Web links to
make sure they're safe, active sites—so encourage your readers to check them out!

Through the Mail or by Phone

ADLER PLANETARIUM AND ASTRONOMY MUSEUM
1300 South Lake Shore Drive
Chicago, IL 60605-2403
312/922-STAR

NATIONAL AIR AND SPACE MUSEUM
7th and Independence Avenue, S.W.
Washington, DC 20560
202/357-2700

LUNAR AND PLANETARY INSTITUTE
3600 Bay Area Boulevard
Houston, TX 77058
281/486-2139

The solar system

Index

About the Author

Charnan Simon has a B.A. in English literature from Carleton College and an M.A. in English literature from the University of Chicago. She began her publishing career in Boston, in the children's book division of Little, Brown and Company. She also spent six years as an editor at *Cricket* magazine before becoming a full-time author. Simon has written more than 40 books for kids, and numerous magazine stories and articles. In addition to writing and freelance editing, she is also a contributing editor for *Click* magazine. Simon lives in Madison, Wisconsin, with her husband Tom, their daughters, Ariel and Hana, Sam the dog, and Lily and Luna the cats.